OPENED WINDOWS
A BOOK OF POEMS

BY:
MIGUEL A. CUELLAR

Published by
Miguel A. Cuellar
Brownsville, Texas, 78521

Text © 2022 by Miguel A. Cuellar
Illustrations © Douglas Brown
www.albumartist.com

Paperback ISBN Number 979-8-218-67253-9

Library of Congress Catalog Number TXu 2-345-257
Library of Congress Catalog Number TXu 2-345-228
Library of Congress Catalog Number TXu 2-344-304
Library of Congress Catalog Number TXu 2-344-361
Library of Congress Catalog Number TXu 2-344-320

Designed © 2025 by RGV Media Group: Jason Moody
Print and Online

Printed in the USA

INTRODUCTION

"Opened Windows," A Book of Poems & Illustrations. The best of two worlds. Lifelong memories, acute observations, creations of metaphoric visions and trends of conceptual thought based on reality, all brought to life in their final form.

Opened Windows is a vivid transcription and visualization that demonstrates how the past, present, and future are alive and well.

Table of Contents

Ocean Blue

Find me an ocean with endless blue
where glistening light shimmers beyond its view
Where sand dollars dot crystal shores
and the warm wind is an embrace
Here in this place I could spend some time
Where I would feel safe to dream
To dream a ship in full sails
That would gently lift me over the swells
And steadfast rise to the ends of the earth
Bringing me back to my place of birth
Where all is well, there are no walls and nowhere to fall
Not to think twice this ocean of endless blue
Is where I'll surely stay

In The Beginning

Never a beginning
Dormant in forever past
So blissful the unknowing
Creation itself awaits

With your beginning
you'll awaken soon
Your vision comes to light
The journey must begin

Reaching out with illumination
Portals of vision are opened
Everywhere, your eyes reach out
Choose a path and venture forth

Fear not what you find
What you see is only you
As you go, your steps will show
Forever your only guide

And though you may never return
Your past will always be
You came from perfect peace
May your destiny be whole again

Set in motion, you're a witness of life
Never again the beginning
Thereafter, your purpose is born
Lifes' journey, lifes' creation

Never To End

SOS I Love You

Escape your world and live forever again
Dream of never growing old and wondering when
With you I'll live and love you, over and over again

Understand, I can't say, you're feeling there's no way
Wondering if it's OK, who'll be first, don't delay
Sight on seen, I'll be the one to see you through

It's easy to say, forever I will love you
The truth and I, your soul renewed
Sight on seen, I'll never let you go

Escape your world and live forever again
Dream of never growing old and wondering when
With you I'll live and love you, forever again

The Painter

With many ways
The crest of life awaits
And with every day
my eyes awaken

The colors begin to shift
wondering where they lay
As the canvas peers
in need of display

The unfinished pallet
Looks for its place
Gradually reaching
for more color in its space

Too much red
or not enough brown
Looking too blue
or too far down

I'll stroke my colors gently
And blend my shades with care
And in perfect light
The shadows will fall

The Lighthouse

I shall live in a lighthouse
    for all of time
Placing light in the dark
    when you're hoping to find
I know where you're going
    you'll never arrive
You're already there
    you too must survive
I'll give you a beam of light
    and throw in a scheme
Then send you on your way
    forever in my dream
Always remember, my light
    throughout time will be
See with my eyes
    then you too will find
The Lighthouse and me

Opened Windows

Curious the mind, an opened window
Free to see other realms
In your thoughts a space within
The vision dwells
Witness this foreign space
So close but still so far
Yet familiar it seems
A place revealed, an awakened dream
And as time sways in and out
Your summoned visions become real
Where many views are concealed
A truth be told
An answer lies waiting
Where you alone will perceive
As your mind breaks free
Through opened windows

A Bridge In Tuscany

"Countess Matilda, your command is my wish"
common this man that gently spoke
"Pardon my presence in the warmth of your spas
a speedy dismissal is in order"

"I think not," she spoke, "I must know your name"

"Yes my countess. Julian that I may serve"

"Then serve me with the pleasure of your company
I wish to know you well"

And Long the night of love and starlit whispers

"Julian. The Serchio River runs between us
My Castle Canossa and spas, leave us divided
So empty they will seem without you
Reaching across the river, I will build a bridge
Bringing castle and spas together
For you and I, merely a short walk away
Again, the warmth of these waters will be ours"

A bridge with beauty and mystery unknown
Canossa Castle to The Spas of Matilda
Matilda of Tuscany and her love for Julian
The need and love of heart and soul

"Julian. Nothing between us ever again
For a thousand years our love will live on
I will Christen our story, The Bridge of Mary Magdalene
In Her name, the vision of our love"

And with their love, all along the way
this love as so it may seem
Matilda and Julian's Bridge, and the river between
A bridge unknown, a bridge conceived

One thousand years
and yet one thousand more
Blessed from above
A bridge made of love

A Bridge In Tuscany

Lovers of Light

We came to this world
in search of our birth
To roam these lands
Grounds of Mother Earth
With a beam of light
shining through our eyes
Lighting our paths
that crossed through our lives
We feared our bodies
but we knew the unknowing
Nurturing our minds
with the light that was glowing
Our destiny forming
Gods' love with our plight
And with only our need
growing stronger with our light
A reunion as one
Changing time in our embrace
The beauty of our love
Changing living into grace
Our light so forgiving
The miracle of living
We are lovers of light

Tibet's Vision

Mountainous wondrous vistas
Sheer unblemished beauty
Majestic upheaval of power and grace
residing above the clouds
Placed in splendor over lands unseen
Realms unknown, records withhold
Contemplation in the endless expanse
Pondering the arrival of space and time

Tibet of old, plateaus of awareness
Therein, follow The Enlightened Ones
To usher in the vision of Tibet
Fostered by the light the ancient sage is born
To administer a body of structure
The creation of Universal Harmony
With ancient records transcribed
and the metaphysical revealed
Brings rise a pilgrimage of the highest order
Destined through the generations
The sage of time is self proclaimed
Profession of The High Priest
A Tibetan belief, The Tibetan Way

Twilight of men, bastions of the light
God's way of sharing the sanction of His life
A union brought forth with a gentle spirit
Healing of the heart, mind and soul
A physical continuum balancing light and dark
    life and death, love and war
Settling the wounds of primal conflicts
Diminishing disdain for compassion
Bearing deep seated cause with reason
These endeavors, never to let go

Tibet's journey will always be
A faith in the souls of many
A path taken with hearts as one
Governance of common good
A message uniting love and life
An endless walkway of light
Eternal bridge anchored in stone
Steadfast arches of light
Suspended in space and time
Land of the high, these magic mountains
Where High Priests are born
Lay witness The Sage Of Old
Comes The Order of Tibet's Vision

The Calm Glow Of White Fire

In a realm without form lays a glow
There lays an ember that shines without light
In a timeless space, origins unknown
An ancient relic of time

The dark needs the glow, so the ember grows
And reaching for the light, a flame appears
a flame of white fire
An ageless lantern of light

The flame flickers at the darkness
The construction of light, and so it begins
Lite-toned shades of color appear
A primal passage through the dark

The domain of life awakens
The self knowing of life set in motion
And with only a glowing ember
  and the dark's need for light

So ignites the spark of creation
The building blocks of life
In all it's everlasting ways
And so is - The calm glow of white fire

The Scribe

The word, light as air
Ethereal whisps of sound
Subscribed from the mind's eye
Dreams awakened, etched in clay

The spoken word lost
Time stands empty, history erased
An innocent self portrayal
All at the will of the scribe

Immortality is now in reach
A signatures found on tablets of stone
The law written through the ages
The scribe remembered through history's past

Daunting this task at hand
Witness if you will
A natural order suspended
Forward moves the force of the scribe

The written word changes, again and again
Changing from king to king
from scribe to scribe
Bribe after bribe the laws obscured

God's commandments will rise over lies
Confusion surrenders to clarity
Laws written by men rendered useless
And the scribe prevails

Unequivocal, the eternal law
The word, written in stone
Never changed or forever lost
And yet today our lives

At the will of The Scribe

The Light Within

Mountains dream in the skies, while deep oceans sleep
Night and day, day and night, the swirling earth
within far reaching countless suns
Plunging through space, a falling spiro of time

All corners of the earth thriving with life
We've roamed the lands beyond all horizons
Landscapes filled with wonder and danger
And the night proceeds the dawn

Subjects to our journey hard won
Where fears are born and the will grows strong
Our days grow short as our nights grow long
And all paths taken must end

The search for salvation begins, surely there is a God
Why His face so hidden, patron of eternal life
Look upon me and revive me with your light
Allow not my path to end

Take not the time you need, to bless yourself with fortune
God's relevance is present amongst the many
Already your life is one with God
The light you seek is the light within

Passage Through The Dark

The light of fire shows the way
It feels as though it takes your fear
It lets you know to chase it's warm glow and draw you near
And suddenly leaves you cold

From nothing comes nothing, the light will take and grow
From light comes the light, leaving darkness so it can glow
Rise Dominion, leave pain, screaming darkness fall
From this loss the light will reign, the light bares no shame

From nothing comes nothing, taking life and leaving death
Cast in need to search and seek, life's every single breath
Forever searching, nowhere in sight, darkness in the light
With our only choice remains, Passage Through The Dark

The light of fire shows the way
It feels as though it takes your fear
It lets you know to chase it's warm glow and draw you near
And suddenly leaves you cold

Love And Hate

The promise of love, the dread of hate
Love and Hate, as they greet hand in hand
"How have you been," they snicker
Again we meet and our story must be told

They both agree, face to face
in all the days gone by
"You remind me so, how I used to be"
"I know you well, you were once me"

We are more alike than not
How every time it seems
Always trying to take us apart
As if such a bad dream

Ice and fire, snow and the far away sun
Melting the cold for spring
Opposing forces, bearing blossoms of life
Never ending treasures prevail

We play the day with all who we are
Be it love or hate we'll struggle
One for all and all for one
This drama will never end

And the fight stands worthy
Where losers are always remembered
And winners are blessed with vision
The tale of life remains

So we go, forward we move
My old nemesis, my old friend
Let us stay hand in hand
This age old struggle is ours to keep

Our union of love and hate
Just as well, our old story
Reason enough, peace and war
Our path seems so clear

In all the days gone by
You remind me so, how I used to be
I know you well, you were once me
And our story must be told

The Word

If God can move worlds
He's moved one too many
or one not enough

God's Heaven On Earth

In time past, not so long ago
hidden in the annals of time
God governed the land
Stories in ancient script
the governance of God on earth

The land and seas were rich with life
Crystal blue skies and shimmering rain
The earth complete with plenty to share
An endless source for all
Divine this gift from God

Soon enough, arose the grievance of life
No longer enough, men became stale
God's presence and counsel transpired
Paradise lay ready to fall
And eternal life was denied

Bad times for men, the good long forgotten
gone with the siege of time
And would not change if not with God
As it was in heaven, was on earth
So now the tree of life awaits

Climb the branch and peer back in time
Invite your soul to see this land of old
Again give rise to common cause
The path is clear, the vision is yours
A world of God with men is real

And if your will allows, this story told
Even a moment well show
this story of old obscured
The governance of God with men
In time past, not so long ago

God's Heaven On Earth

Hail The King

Hail The King, give him what's his
He'll take it fair and square
Dare to keep what you can't hold
it belongs to Him alone
All your toil and even your life
you've given it all away
Part with what you've earned
Live or die, your life or learn
So be it, Hail The King
He too was once like you
Many have tried and died
But only one can see it through
He will not be denied
His journey long and hard
And at the end
the sword will always win
Hail The King
He too was once like you
The golden crown
belongs to Him alone
Hail The King
He was once like you
Hail The King

Standing On The Weak Side of Strength

Look up look down, look all around
is there a way to say
Entwined amongst Gods' space
is it love or is it life
And if I asked Him so
I think He'd mean to say
Welcome to my world, but first you must know
you're standing on the weak side of strength

Do you think this world and many others
so lost at such a cost
Would call a task for fluffy doves
and blessings from above
Or can you see the hand that reigns
is a loving master for souls in pain

Yes my God, I think I know
This side of strength
is not a dove at all for such a fall
I shouldn't think or justify
or even know if I can try
I see there are no dues
or even love that I could buy

Your word my God will be forever
What is said and done will always be
Allow me to bow in your presence
Allow my appeal of submission
For I am Standing on The Weak Side of Strength

Sophia - Goddess of Love

You've never known another way
with your never ending mind
Patiently, waiting out all the days

Searching the endless skies
Determined to live on
to every world you would fly

And such a cost, your ways unknown
How sad to find your lands upset
Riding loves crest above and alone

Be as you may
I need not ask, I know why
All my love I pray

Leaving streaks of light afar
Determined to love on
Waiting by every star

You knew there was still a place
With your never ending will
you found God's grace

See our lands and choose
At any cost, your ways unknown
This world is yours to use

Be as you may
I need not say
All my love and sorrow

Where The Days Are Few

How it is, our time and space bygone
falling through the strands of life
Held as the living, to witness the beginning
A design of unbreachable bonds
We go on thinking, simply thinking
so natural the days are few
We make our way with merely hope
and our vision remains enclosed
Did something so wrong make it worse
or something so good would do as well
Where hidden reality would test anyone's will
Yet the truth remains so hard to see
who would know but from the hereafter
but amongst us all
Naturally, all along the way
our time and space bygone
Where the days are few

Forever Belongs To Never Again

Further and further beyond
You hold on to suspicion
A warning you claimed
Offerings were seen the same

An open end awaits
Holding on to silence
Placing yourself in refrain
Where doubt becomes a game

Can I again be so sure
I see a simple wish
Never again, so unkind
And forever always belongs

At the end
With all destinies thereof
Forever will stand alone
Forever Belongs To Never Again

The Veil Upon Us

How it is, the mystery of life
as far as we can see a mystery at all
Lays hidden a veil
Subduing our vision from a simple truth
An act of mercy unnoticed
A veil placed over our eyes
Saving us from a blinding light
Saving us from the mysterious truth
The mystery of life
The veil upon us
And so must remain the hidden mystery
As far as we can see a mystery at all

Time

Ageless in the vast expanse of space
Encompassing all and everything
Realms that couldn't divide nor records withhold
Noncompositional state of trance

An unseen presence with an immeasurable force
A shapeless image without color
Concealed in its depth and scope
Barely defined and never found

Alternative realms where time conspires
not held, removed or altered
Reality will not adhere
A mystery obscured in vagueness

Time has always been and always will
To the ends of the earth and beyond the stars
Never a beginning, never an end
And everything in between

Forever ageless, time just had to be
Once upon a time
Time and time again
Throughout eternity

Forever Time

Lone Soldier

Lone Soldier, you are not alone
They hear your cadence well
Waiting for your march of silence
Move on towards the light

No time for rest, fall in, forward
Busy your days and nights as one
The mission is clear, a union of soldiers
Lone Soldier, you are not alone

Lead the way with your silent march
Watchmen of soldiers, look over them well
Your breath of life is upon them
They feel the beat of your heart

Move them along lone soldier
Ready the march, soon you'll arrive
Forward in silence with the light
Forward on Lone Soldier

You are not alone

The Scaffold

How high is the sky
What I see can't be
Is this our tragic end
Was this really ever meant to be
Surely madness is on the rise
My time is near to scale the sky
Just a while back it seemed so clear
And now the moment is near
My courage wanes as the scaffold awaits
And my destiny is summoned
To continue on, testing my will
Higher and higher I climb
Will I dare look down
I've passed the point of no return
I'll catch my breath and move on
A place beyond the clouds waits for me
The scaffold becomes a dense weave
Trestles appear piercing the sky
Inconceivable configured design
Succumbing the earth and stars
A masterpiece of light
Eons in the making, as far as the eye can see
Halfway between heaven and earth
Blinded and mind struck with awe
Good God, allow my soul the strength
To bare witness this creation
To complete this journey of life
My eyes lay open
Filled with the unimagined
Crystalline radiance
Ageless construction of light
A statement so absolute
A signature beyond creation
Surely, who am I to say
But simply The Face of God

Ancient Sailor

Ninety days sailing
Dawn and the first streak of light
Yells from the watchman - land ahoy,
ready the anchor, half mast the sails

Pristine beaches await our arrival
Busy our days stocking ballast and bounty
Our decks will lay full with all this land offers
Our stay will be short, uncharted waters await

To this island of refuge, an oasis of life
The winds in our sails were full
Tracking our way by starlit skies
The candle light opera of night

This island laid lost and unknown
A haven found for deep sail waters
Not the end or beginning
and the surging seas never recede

Land locked waters that never subside
Perhaps oceans that will never end
Or the river of life winding through the stars
Weigh the anchors, ready the sails, our passage prevails

We'll sail by the star maps of night
and rest by the light of day
We ask the sea to make us her own
We pray these waters our way back home

Magi Where Are You

Magi disguised in the sands of time
Where upon the silk road did you arrive
Did you open a door from above
And descend amongst men

Magi in disguise, you sought this road
The road of fortune and far away lands
Silk, gold and jewels
An oasis of riches there for you

And in your possession, ancient secrets of life
A higher knowledge unknown
Healing are deepest fears
With the science of body and soul

The Magician, High Priest of Magic
An unreachable craft
You bartered for the healing of men
You traded for the cleansing of sin

Your price for life turned into vast treasure
But where is your written word
Was it ours to ever keep
Or is it lost with demise in the sands of time

Magi in disguise, you planned your exit so well
You gathered your riches and ran
Ascending through your opened door above
And your written word was yours to keep

Magi, your name is in The Sands of Time
Again you came and went
With the power and secrets of life
Again you transcended death

Magi, High Priest of The Sands of Time

Queen Mother of The Heavens

How is one to live
Without the means to love thee well
To know I am without and cannot give
Where even the dark is rendered helpless
When darkness lays waste aside your light
All the while, to witness the rise of Thine Being

Relentless compounding resilience
Defying description, resignation of the word
Canceling the mere laws of life
And with barely a glance, all that remains
is to hold life tried at constant judgment
for its existence alongside your being

Majesty of life transcended
Allow your rise above the misfortune of time
Laid forsaken by its tragedy
That time itself will pay heed
To your lawful possession
Of Thine Jewelian - State of Being

Tales Of The Hunter

Early dawn, the first streak of light
Screaming prey of the night are silent
The unknowing dark passes through
And the clan stirs ready another day

Tribesmen and hunters gather
to tell the stories of yesterday
Their tales of life and death
A life, in the tales of the hunter

Sky Gods look upon us now
Our kill today will be hard won
Armed and ready the beast is strong
We will both stand at the cliff of life

If our spears fall short
and the last arrow is flung
It is then we will know
this beast was not ours to have

If I'm the one not to return
in my hunt for life
Remember well my hunt with death
I was strong and brave will be my story

Do not say I passed short of breath
My stance was firm to the end
Serve well our children with courage
and tell my story of yesterday

The tale of life and death
The Tales Of The Hunter

Michael Archangel

Guardian of the realm
Michael Archangel, say unto me
Allow me to hear your whisper
Your story is yet unknown
Time cannot weigh the measure of your being
Simply, God's body and soul
His manifestation of light
From your radiant golden heart
And your sword of truth in hand
Lives the power bestowed upon your works

"Remorse for those who will go it alone
The sadness wears heavy"
But if salvation is in your reach
The Archangel Michael watches all
May God's enlightenment be upon us
Our path will be narrow, allow us not to waiver
Salvation is weighed in the moment

Redeemer of souls, last bastion of light
Your rise to Supreme Power
Entrusted by God, Supreme Commander
Allow us your story
Fulfillment of the law lays beyond faith
May your merciful heart see us through
Our souls filled with the eternal light
We ask of you in humble prayer
Our passage and salvation

Again The End

Millenniums bygone, only fragments remain
A people concealed with ageless stone
Buried in sand, dust and time
and our past remains a question

An ancient site that has no name
A forgotten world left behind
Lives lived, dispersed in burials
Our past recorded in sacrificial tombs

The rise of Kings, Queens and Gods
Winners and Losers with great wars throughout
Taking spoils and treasure of the captured
Our past locked in time, never to change

Again and again the end, crumbling stone
Ruins into grains of sand
Ash of the flames, bits and pieces still holding on
Another age in time pays its toll

Looking back, the past seems not our own
As we move towards our future unknown
Clearly the horizon seems free of ruin
But yet again, becomes the end

Again The End

Dark Star

Dark Star. You lurk quietly in the black
I've heard and I must ask, what have you done
Common the man in disbelief
I hear you've captured a thousand suns
Their light forsaken, yours to keep
Least your ways eons ago
Design in part of a master plan
Now, with no light to show
go as you may, you cannot hide
At last in the dark you're found
Triumph not, forever cannot be
Your light restrained and bound
Safekeep the light, for soon enough
Never the light, you are the night
Self imposed, self fulfilled
You thought forever you could hold on
Your work is done, the light and dark as one
Locked away for a moment in time
Your captured suns will slip away
And soon, again you will shine
Again we'll see what you have been
Again we'll know what was never shown
And if our days should end
And all we know grows quiet
The truth in you forever known
You are tomorrow's light
You are the star of night
Dark Star

Essence of Love

Love so evasive in shape and form
It's pureness stands alone
A presence unseen
An immeasurable solution
Revealed with silence and peace
Touching all in its path
Soothing hearts and souls
Endless unbreakable bonds
Where even wars have ceased
Simply sharing a gesture
A symbol of friendship
An alliance for the better good
The fall and rise of dominions
The creation of legends
Boundless in power
Yet subtle and gentle
The mystery of love
Perhaps not a mystery at all
Giving of self without condition
Life given for another
Love will never die
No mountain too high or ocean too deep
Finding purpose with reason
Life with love so forgiving
Embodied with the light of love
The essence of your soul
Glistening spirits abound
With the miracle of life
The mystery of love
Warmth of a never-ending glow
The beauty and grace of living

Prayer Of My Soul

Master of Light, Master of Life
Allow me this prayer my Lord and God
You have shared the knowing of your being
And life is a celebration
You brought order to this world awry
With your vision of love and peace
You replaced chaos and disdain
With your life amongst men
And for the works You have provided
My words of thankfulness can never be enough
So allow me to be guided throughout
With your design of life and love
Dearest Father, Prince of Peace
The path I walk, the words I speak
Enlightened I shall be, the truth I will see
I am not to forget this gift of life
That you so willingly shared
Allow me to embrace righteous ways
With a life of love and peace
This life is a celebration
I am grateful and I am blessed
I am fortunate and I feel forgiven
For allowing me to know
The presence of Your Being

In God We Trust

Long ago and maybe so far
someone created a story
Brought from a place oh so old
He's sure to have his glory
Not just a game so many have played
Not just a tale so many have told
About Kings and Queens and all their affairs
as God and His Works unfold
Ancient scripts written in tongues
The story of God written by men
And all who claim the enlightened ones
One by one, time and again
Let there be light with a jewel sheen
Birth of our vision darkness redeemed
Redemption with light, awakened souls
The essence of living, forgiving your need
Here to announce the chosen one
Here to receive your treasure of gold
Witness now my life of wealth
Tabernacle of God, altar of stone
Let it be known, the story of light
The Word Enshrined
In God We Trust

My Old Friend Once Again

Along the way, far and beyond
Can't remember when
Saw your face in the stars
With just a moment's glance
It was just enough to stir my soul
I'd like to see you then
Then and now my friend
Vision from afar, come to me
Come to me so I can see
My Old Friend Once Again

A Musicians Creed

I am drawn towards your vastness,
                              for you cannot be defined
I see your arena, staged and aligned
Conductor of Life, a song I hear
Eminence of music, you rid me of fear
Constructing a scaffold, the foundation is laid
Preludes the Entro as the melody is played
The vision unfolds in true exposition
The signature is written without condition
And my attempt with the music you withhold
is the treasure you share, as your story is told

Push me and use me, guide me with sound
Take me and send me with the will of your song
Your infinite ways with orchestrations
You are the Magistrate of Symphonies
The blessing of song
Changing life into music
You are Lord of The Singing Crown

Mirror Mirror It Was Always You

Mirror mirror, just once I ask
I need to know your ways
Again and again, there's nothing to see
Over and over, it's always me

Stories of fortune and tales so tragic
Tricks revealed or genuine magic
Seeing misfortune, the future at stake
Do or die, make or break

So your story goes
Hearsay mysteries, the stuff of legend
A mainstay of fascination
But the mirror and me is all I see

Mirror mirror again and again
Over and over you've seen me well
The whole time knowing
Mirror mirror, it was always you

The Circus

Carousels wavering and winding, under cover of night
Destination unknown, seeking days first light
Peering out for in common space, their arrival awaits
Swayed by a magical force, to an illusive place

Uncertain for the circus escapades
Expressionless, as the clowns charade
Dampened costumes, poised for rerun shows
The audience bewildered, as the story is told

Midgets and elephants, together on stage
Gypsies and tigers, showing love and rage
Center stage brings hope for the trapeze stranger
Screaming joy when there's no more danger

And the juggler never sees but the pins he throws
If he drops just one, it'll ruin the show
He can always try again, he's safe on the ground
He'll do another trick and take your frown

Tame the lion as he snarls and fights
As he jumps through fire, it's his only right
Caged, restrained and defiled
The lion looks as if standing trial

The polar bear grumbles, as he plays catch with the seal
"We're both from the arctic, how is this real"
Magic from a hat, rabbits turned into doves
Everyone is wondering, is it life or love

And off in a cannon, someone's thrown with a blast
Flying he seems, into the show he is cast
From beauty to the beast, to the Kings and Queens
From a purr to a roar, this can't be a dream

Step right up, take the best seat in town
Enjoy the spectacle, we'll see you next time around
Come one Come all
To The Greatest Show On Earth

Someone's Peering Through My Eyes

I see the earth and sky
though my world it seems unknown
A stranger in my home
Someone's peering through my eyes

Somewhere along the way
Awakened my soul I pray
With my eyes to see us through
And if not my soul, then who

Now and then I cease to notice
in hopes my eyes will clear
And then again, at a glance
Someone's there I fear

Imagination with observations
forever changing my view
One in the same, I think I know
forever I question if true

Does one understand between truth and lies
Someone's peering through my eyes

Waltzed In Stone

Talk to me, hold on to me
You've been living on the edge
All the while you knew
Tell me if you can

I heard you were seen
Gently dancing on the cliff
Your partner was fate itself
Old friends happy again

A freedom so pure
No rhyme or reason
The beginning and end as one
A greater expanse lay witness

I thought I heard you
whisper in my ear
"If you can see the edge
you'll see my gentle dance"

Dance with me, let us waltz
on the cliffs of stone
Your time has come
And I'm still here

Here for you, simply free
The beginning and end
Dancing with fate
Forever in a day

Waiting to gently steer you
away from the edge
Just close enough to see
Dancing forever away

A signature inscribed
I'll see you through
Where your dance too
Will be Waltzed In Stone

Sky Blue

Let the day go, embrace the night
Welcome shadows of dusk
See off with a smile last rays of light
Tomorrow must wait tonight

One by one the stars will appear
In the dark of night, a thousand sparkles
Your bewildered vision welcomes their light
The gift of darkness, so forgiven

Sky blue is now, light in the dark
A blanket of warmth with a dim glow
Let the day go embrace the night
I see your star so clear

Sky blue, I'll always love you
But tonight there's no tomorrow
Forever you and I in the silence of night
I embrace you, skylight of the dark

Sky blue, I'll always love you

In memory of Skye Blue

Allow Me The Privilege.

During the pandemic lockdown, my beloved and long-lived Husky, Sky Blue, was ready to pass on.

As I lay with her, my mind stirred with beautiful memories, narrated with silent captions. Writing them down, little did I know, it would be the first composed entry, written in this body of poems.

With plenty of time and inspiration, I began continuously writing. About four months later, it just stopped. Sky Blue had moved my entire life with her passing. In her honor, I ended my book with her poem - "Sky Blue."

Miguel A. Cuellar, AKA Mick, was born and reared in Brownsville, Texas, attending private Catholic schools and local junior college. Currently, retired after a long career as a performing musician, general maintenance, and residential property management. After 36 years residing in Austin, Texas, he has relocated to Brownsville, to be with family & to walk the shores of South Padre Island.

Artist Bio

Douglas Brown was born in Panama City, Panama. He and his family moved to Austin, Texas, at an early age where he continues to live and work. Mr. Brown attended the University of Texas at Austin and graduated with a degree in art, focusing on painting. After being commissioned by the City of Austin and a number of other businesses to create murals, he taught himself computer- based design and founded Album Artist.

At Album Artist, he combined his passions for art and music, working with local musicians and venues to produce promotional material and album covers. Eventually, Mr. Brown expanded his operations to work with local businesses producing brochures, logos and other sales materials.

When Hollywood started coming to town, Mr. Brown mixed his love of drawing and movies and began offering storyboard services to the local film community. He has since worked with national clients such as iRobot, Perry Ellis, Wendy's, GE, MTV, Trojan-ENZ, Domino's Pizza, and other production companies.